The Ramblings of a Cumbrian Heathen

A Collection of Poems

By Tom Higgins

The Ramblings of a Cumbrian Heathen

A Collection of Poems

All contents copyright © 2013 – Tom Higgins

Dedication

To my three wonderful girls.

Contents

Introduction

Hello my name is Tom Higgins and at the time of publication, I am fifty-nine years old, married with two daughters. We shall have been married for thirty years on 30th July this year!

I had never written more than a postcard since I left school at the age of seventeen, but about three years ago I was watching a documentary about the shortage of water in certain parts of the planet which was the prompt which triggered my first attempt at recording my thoughts on the issue.

I have been an avid reader of fiction and history throughout my life, and latterly I have increasingly discovered a growing interest in some of life's great mysteries which provides me with a method of ensuring that I am never bored as the ever expanding library of man's scientific discoveries is now easily accessed from anywhere on the planet where a laptop or any other device can connect to the internet.

I do have a view of the world as a very contradictory place where great beauty can be found sometimes a stone's throw from wickedness and violence, and I try to reflect this in some of what I write. There are other great absurdities which I like to question, and some people find that they don't like anyone asking such questions, but that road leads to tyranny so I will keep on asking.

I have posted some of my work on some poetry sites, and I have had good feedback in general except from the academically trained "poets", who seem to find fault with everything I write, because I know nothing of the vast array of different styles of word play that make up" poetry" in their very well educated world. The problem is I can understand very little of what these people write. I feel that they have created an exclusive club in which only those who have been given access to the codes can comprehend what it is they are saying. I write to tell short stories that people other than myself can understand. I do not write poetry to win prizes for technical brilliance. I write to express what I am thinking and feeling at a given moment and feelings are not taught in any educational establishment. I try use language that all those who have not had the privilege to be classically educated can read and understand with ease.

So if you decide that this is of interest to you, and you partake of a copy of this, my first anthology then thank you I hope you enjoy reading my poems!

Kindest Regards,

Tom Higgins
April 2013

REVEILLE

The sunrise is a golden peach delight

Melting the treacle blackness

Of the kingdom of the night.

The brightening wakens me

From my deep insensible slumber,

And outside of my window

The songbirds grow in number

To sing their dawn chorus

Competing to be heard

Each big boy trying to sing much louder,

Than any other big boy bird.

So the conspiracy of our brilliant star,

And my feathered cocky friends,

Means that now it's very certain

This is where my snoozing ends!

WHERE IS KNOWLEDGE BORN?

There is so much information all around,

And pearls of wisdom can be found

Everywhere on this internet,

But with all my seeking I have not yet

Found the source, she is such an elusive girl

That fount of all knowledge the Mother of Pearl!

A Secret Little Prayer

Although I don't believe in God,

I always find that I,

Say a little secret prayer,

Before venturing into the sky!

Yes, every time I board a plane,

I offer up some words,

I don't believe anyone's there to listen,

And I don't believe they're heard.

But, as I clip on the safety belt,

And watch the cabin crew,

Showing us, what, if things go wrong,

Just what we have to do.

I offer up my secret little plea,

That if there's something there to care,

Then look after my fellow passengers and me,

And keep this bloody thing in the air!

Now I know that I'm a hypocrite,

I don't need it pointed out,

But I'm not as bad as those Godly men,

Who hate, and scream, and shout.

At those who won't do as they say,

Who refuse to accept their rules,

Who will not bend to life their way,

Who won't become suffering fools!

GOD LOG STARDATE THIRTEEN BILLION

I watched more people starving,

down on planet Earth today,

but I decided not to bother,

this is how I like to play.

One off against the other,

the strong against the weak,

the haves against the have nots,

who have no voice to speak.

THE REMOVAL MEN

The thought police, for the thinkers came,

they took them all in one night.

It was time for them to extinguish enlightenment's

flame,

to consolidate and make greater the might,

of the powerful clique, the scheming few,

who'd combined to usurp all power,

and now the time of retribution came, to,

all who disagreed, or whose thoughts did tower,

above those of the ruling menace,

who feared these ideas would spread,

so they removed them from the human race,

attempting to stop their questions, dead!

A QUESTION OF MORALITY

Surprise! Surprise!

Another banker lies.

The people he robs

Of their wealth and jobs,

Are left to wonder,

to ask how they,

Have to, for years,

To continue to pay,

Whilst the high placed

Thieves walk away,

With the fruits of their

Deception and theft.

What does this tell us

About our world?

Is there any morality left?

PISCINE PHILOSOPHY

My goldfish waits patiently to be fed,
he waits without moving much.
When I approach, what goes through his head,
does he actually think thought patterns or such?
He gets excited as I take some food
and sprinkle it into the tank,
does he look up to me as his one true god,
the father that all fishkind must thank,
for being there each and every day
to make sure all his needs I'll meet,
does he look up to me and pray
that forever, I'll make sure he'll eat?

CHANCES ARE?

The likelihood of seeing,

a non-terrestrial, intelligent, being,

who greets you with a friendly wave, and,

announcing that his name is Dave,

he then asks you to take him to your leader,

is about as probable as hearing,

that the day is actually nearing,

when equality and fairness,

replace the general, couldn't care less

attitude which today is rather prevalent,

and which is actually quite malevolent.

What do you think,

dear reader?

IF LEFT TO THINK FOR ONESELF.

The seed of the Jewish man,

Swims frantically towards its goal,

To be united with that Muslim egg,

To unite in the creation of a soul,

A human child that is the same,

As any other on the Earth,

Until it is born, when begins the daft game,

From the moment of its birth.

This child is a Muslim says the mother,

No it is a Jew says the dad,

If the child had a say would it not think of other,

Than these two choices, both sad ?

REACH OUT AND TOUCH SOMEBODY'S WALLET.

On Friday night whilst I, in boredom,
was channel hopping
Through lots of rubbishy programs,
including shopping.

I regret to admit that I found me
Reached out to and touched by satellite, God TV.
Lots of pop singers and glamour there, and a message
for all the lost young kids to share,
Oh it's so good to be good, and how they really,
really care.

Then came the request to every person
who feels they can
To give as much money as possible,
to help their fellow man.

Now call me cynical, but questions do arise
Who actually gets the cash, and would it be wise,
For me to simply shrink the size of my bank account,
to give it to
Someone who preaches one thing, but who,
Is really in it for their own gain?
Leaving those in need to retain their pain.

Smiley, smiley, yes indeed, we are true believers
of our creed.
No other people have ever been so truly freed,
Can't you see that clearly all other beliefs are wrong?
That we are oh so right, and we are also very strong.

So follow us and sing out loud for the salvation
of your soul,

Join us on our journey, and we will mend the hole,

In your life that you really need to have filled.

Before any hope within you ends up being killed!

It would be nice to believe they do it solely

for the cause,

But unfortunately, my time on Earth,

makes me take a pause

To weigh up all the pros and cons of each

and every offer,

Especially those supposedly from God which the keys

to Heaven proffer.

I only know that this dream of a God has been around

since history began,

And that he or she never existed before the

consciousness of man!

THE TRILOGY OF DUPLICITY

The god of Moses and Abraham
is now divided into three,
not Father, Son and Holy Ghost as was taught
to little old me.
But because Muslim, Christian and Jewish men have
got it into their heads,
that the deity belongs to them,
despite the common threads.
And so it seems the spread of hate will drive our
destiny and fate,
for it is easier for the lazy mind to be told what to think
and so remain blind,
than to question, just a wee, how one god,
can become three?
Or even how, if everything that is must have a maker,
did their god come to be?
Perhaps some universal master baker?

CAN YOU SEE THE COOKIE TREE?

I was walking in the park last week,

when to me, a young boy did speak.

'Excuse me mister can you tell me,

where can I find a cookie tree?

I know that there are some in here,

and I've been told that they are near,

yes, before I was the age of three,

I knew all about the cookie tree!

I've never seen one yet, although,

they're definitely here, yes this I know,

as from a very young age they've told me so,

that cookie trees in this park grow.

So come on mister, tell me please,

where in this park are the cookie trees?

I have to find them before I'm old,

and they're definitely here, because I've been told.'

I answered him in the following way.
'Since I was young I've come to play,
and wander freely all around this park,
but your question leaves me in the dark.
Because, never once in all this time,
have I come across any sign,
to tell me that cookies grow on trees,
where did you get your info please? '
Straight away, the kid replied.
'Oh well, you're the first one that I've tried.
I didn't think I'd do it with ease,
you know, find the orchard of cookie trees.
So I'll carry on until I find,
someone who believes, and isn't blind,
yes a person who really, truly agrees,
with the fact that cookies grow on trees!

OUR TIME TOGETHER WAS GOOD

I wrote these words for you, my friend.

We never know when we'll reach the end.

I only know I'm so proud to say

That I'm so glad you passed my way,

And through our lives you were such a good mate

When times were bad, and when times were great,

And I always knew as time whizzed past

That a true friendship is built to last.

And yet now I stand alone to read

This tribute to a friend, indeed.

As sadness permeates my soul

I feel that I'm no longer whole

That part of what made me, has gone,

I'm left all alone to soldier on

Through what remains of my lifespan

Without you here, a very lonely man.

But my love for you was always so strong,

And that love's power will help me get along.

So my love, my thanks for sharing

Your life with me, and for your caring

Enough for me to see it through,

I only wish that it was not true

That you have now forever gone,

My one true love the only one.

FOR THE GLORY OF?

Those out there who wish to die,

To meet your imaginary friend in the sky,

Please think about the deed you plan,

To kill and maim your fellow man,

And ask why it is that it falls to you,

To see this 'holy' mission through?

When those who trained you, and conceived the story,

Of heavenly virgins, and martyrdom's glory,

Will all remain here both feet on Earth's ground,

Why is it that they never got around,

To strapping on the explosive belt,

How come that they have never felt,

Such powerful urges to be the one,

To go to the market with the bomb strapped on?

Is it perhaps that these older men know,

That there's nowhere after the explosives blow?

And the reason that they've brainwashed you,

Is that you'll do the deed that they'd never do!

It is a fact through man's history,

There is absolutely no mystery,

That when it comes to starting wars,

Those scheming ones who are the cause,

Never turn out on the field of battle,

They just train dogs to herd the cattle!

WHO ATE ALL THE PIES?

It wasn't him, it was his eyes,

That made him eat all the pies.

This is what the fat man said

Just before he dropped down dead.

It was the lard in every pie

That built up inside and made him die.

By filling his arteries till they blocked,

His blood stopped flowing, his body shocked.

His bloated heart no longer beating

All because of what he'd been eating.

Now of course it is too late

To change what went on to his plate.

So all you youngsters who like pies,

Don't be told what to do by your eyes.

Choose the food that does you good

Eat fruit and veg, you know you should.

Then you will live to a ripe old age,

Before you have to exit from life's stage,

And so many people will not be sad,

Because dying old doesn't seem as bad.

As dying when you are still young,

Before your song was even sung.

No, an old age exit is the way out of choice

After the world has heard your voice!

WATERY LOTTERY

Water, as most of you will know,

has the chemical formula H2O.

Now this essential liquid is, as well,

in its natural form, devoid of smell,

and also in its pure state,

it's clear and clean and really great,

for keeping living things alive,

as without it nothing can survive.

Yes it really is such magic stuff,

because without it things are really tough,

and it often makes me stop and think.

each time I pour myself a drink.

What would I do if it all dried up?

Turn on the tap, but an empty cup!

Nothing from the pipes emanating,

panic, as I'm not used to waiting.

This is not how it is for me,

I live where rain falls frequently,

and I can drink, shower and bathe too,

as often as I'm wanting to.

But in other parts it rains only rarely,

and people there, well they can barely,

find enough water for their needs,

to drink, to wash, to nurture seeds.

For them life is infinitely harder,

they've learned to live with an empty larder,

and simple hygiene is so hard to achieve,

when the detritus of living, they have to leave,

lying, rotting, stinking on the surface all around,

polluting any water source in the ground.

Because of the extreme poverty of these 'others',

on my TV screen I have seen the faces of the mothers,

whose children died because there has never been

access to water which is drinkable and clean.

Yes, something that we take for granted,

because we were born, where we were planted!

HEAVEN AND HELL.

There is no Heaven,
There is no Hell.
Only on the minds of men,
Do such places dwell.

There is no monkey Heaven,
There is no Monkey Hell.
And the minds of monkeys
On such places never dwell.

IT HAPPENED NATURALLY!

Big bang happened, time began,

Now here we are, the sons of man,

Discussing whether a supreme being,

Of such might and wisdom all seeing,

Could possibly be around before,

Any time existed, and what's more,

Could pick a tiny isolated planet,

And with a vast array of zoology, man it!

Now that is more than incredible,

If it was pie it would be inedible.

The thought that out of billions of galaxies,

He chose one tiny planet for the people he's,

Made in his own likeness to do his bidding,

No really he must have just been kidding,

And out there among those trillions of stars

There are billions more Earth's, where there are,

Trillions more like you and me,

Discussing how they came to be!

THE MAD HATERS TEA PARTY

I'm gonna have a tea party,
And I will only invite,
Those of you who think like me,
And who with me will unite
In their contempt for the poor
Who we believe are parasites,
And that if you have no money
Then you should have no rights.

No we don't wanna pay taxes
To be squandered on health care
For those who don't contribute,
Who never pay their share!
No matter that they can't find work,
That matters not a jot,
They ain't tryin' hard enough
By god I'm sure they're not!

Yes I'm havin' me a tea party

For all who agree with me,

That poor people are sad losers,

Who don't deserve to be,

Living in our proud nation,

Where the greenback calls the shots,

And the haves feel anger and frustration

About giving anything to the have nots!

A FUNDAMENTAL QUESTION

I have a question, to which so far

My life's experience cannot provide an answer.

How could a benign, thinking, loving,

and caring creator,

Come up with such a thing as cancer?

ON LIVING.

This collective of cells manifests itself to be,

Everything that is seen to be me.

But question then what awareness is,

And, what is it that makes me fizz?

I am not merely a living thing,

What creates the joy to make me sing?

And forms my dreams of those beautiful days,

Of warm sunshine and evening haze,

Of a full moon filling a dark blue sky,

with silvery light to help see by,

Of a gentle breeze blowing meadow flowers,

And rainbows framing summer showers.

Yes there are lots of whats, and whys, and hows,

Growing beside life's pathway on which we browse,

And answers are still so very hard to find,

To the questions raised whilst living by mankind.

I Live One Life.

Why fear death?

With my last breath,

I will be gone forever.

Before my birth,

My only appearance on Earth,

I did not exist, no never!

And so when I die,

There'll be nowhere to fly,

No me left to go,

This I do know,

And I can live with this thought,

As my life it has taught,

That all of life ends,

Even for family and friends,

And this includes me

And it allows me to be free,

Because I'm not scared of dying,

And to myself I'm not lying,

So there's no sense in me,

Pretending that I see,

What just is not there,

For which I don't care.

No, I shall just live,

Love and forgive,

In a life which is good,

As all of us should,

And I'll never concede,

That I need some creed,

To tell me which way,

To live every day,

How I should think,

What I may drink,

What I can eat,

This or that kind of meat.

No, my life choice is mine,

And I live it just fine.

I don't need to believe,

That after death I'll receive,

Access to the Land of Never Never,

Now isn't that cleverer than clever?

That there can be,

Where no man can see,

A place of such infinite glory,

Where the 'good' continue their story,

In some parallel universe,

Unaffected by time's curse,

Somewhere that we,

Can live for infinity,

But only if we truly believe,

In a permanently imaginary divinity!

A WHISPER ON THE BREEZE.

I think I've come to understand,

That most of life goes by unplanned,

And time passes us in such a hurry,

There is no point to doubt and worry,

As nothing is ever as it seems,

Our reality merges with our dreams,

So that every day of life one sees,

Is just a whisper on the breeze.

STATUS QUO

You're born into poverty,

So life is a bitch,

But it's poverty that makes,

Every rich person rich!

THIS RACING LIFE

And they're off, and they've set off at speed
And "New Kid On The Block" takes an early lead,
Quickly followed by "Wide Eyed With Wonder",
And coming up quickly and from under,
The radar is that fast improving colt "Teenage Fear"
On his shoulder comes "Promising Career."
Who is being trailed closely by "New Girlfriend"
Followed closely by "Love Will Never End"

Hot on their heels now comes "Engagement Ring"
Followed closely by "Ding Dong Ding"
And passing them now it's "Marital Bliss"
Swiftly followed by "Babykiss",
Then closely behind comes "Mega Cost",
Neck and neck with "Freedom Lost".
And as they come to the half way mark,
It's "Big Mortgage" followed by "Mistress Dark"

But moving up through the bunch to take the lead now

Is" Divorce Lawyer" moving fast, but wow!

"New Wife" shoots to the front of the fray,

But he's not letting the mare get away,

And as they turn into the finishing straight ,

"Divorce Lawyer" seems to have left it late.

And as they move into the final three furlongs,

Coming up fast as if it's where he belongs,

Is the novice colt "Home Alone" making ground,

But what's this? Out wide moving smoothly round,

It's the rank outsider "Match.Com" and right behind,

Comes, "Russian Beauty" Who seems not to mind,

That she was never in the betting for this race,

As she moved steadily up the field place by place,

She's closely followed by " My Lonely Heart"

Who from halfway has played a very big part

In this exciting race for the line and glory

But today writes "Russian Beauty's" story

As she crosses first to win this Year's race,

Now who thought she'd come in first place?

Into the winners circle on parade,

The handsome mare has now made the grade,

The crowd all comment "she is some looker."

But when the eyes aren't watching, it'll be "so long

sucker!"

MURDERED FOR MY TEETH.

The killing has started again.
They shoot us, and then,
We trumpet our last breath
Then we crumple into death.

The African men,
Who killed us, then,
Hack out our tusks,
Leave us as husks

In the African dust.
But, kill us they must,
As for doing this deed,

They'll be able to feed,

Their children, for a year,

Thus diminishing their fear.

They were paid more

Than they ever saw,

Which made them willing

To do the killing,

Because Chinamen

Carve our ivory, then,

Sell it on to

The nouveau rich,

Those nincompoops who,

Want everything which

Their money can buy.

I hear Mother Earth cry "Stop!"

As gold inflates their vanity

But provides not the tiniest drop

Of any decency or humanity,

To encourage an end to this insanity.

They just live the big lie

That they can simply buy,

The elusive emotion, happiness,

That they think they can possess!

Derived from trinkets and rings

And other silly, shiny and sparkly things.

TWO LITTLE BOYS AND ONE TINY BIRD

I am eight years old, my friend is ten,

The sky is billions and azure blue,

We are walking to St Bees and the beach, when,

Suddenly a skylark soars piping his tune so true.

We watch and listen as the tiny bird,

In undulating flight trills his lovely song,

It is like nothing else that we have ever heard,

And he keeps singing for joy as we continue along

The narrow country lane down to the sea,

Where all day we'll explore the rocky shore

and weedy fronds,

Knowing that there will doubtless be,

Myriads of strange creatures in their salty ponds.

I am fifty seven, my friend is fifty nine,

His health is not so good, but he battles on,

Myself, I am feeling mostly fine,

Although the best years have now gone.

The sky is billions and a bit, and sometimes it is blue,

And as I drive along the still narrow lane

Towards St Bees where skylarks once flew,

The only thing flying in the sky is a tiny silver plane,

And the only sounds come from engine noise,

and BBC Radio Two.

Down on the beach the rocky pools and seaweed

fronds,

All are clearly still there,

But there are not so many animals in their salty ponds,

Did they just vanish into thin air?

Or is it perhaps that I can no longer see,

Through these older, more tired eyes,

The same things I saw when I was young and free,

When every new day would unwrap a totally different

surprise?

FROM HERE TO ETERNITY, ALMOST!

The defining moment in my lifetime so far,

Was the instant I first understood, what we are,

That we've been around since time began,

And that every atom which makes this ape, called man,

Has been part of the mechanism of nature's machine

For countless ages past, and will be for those

not yet seen.

Here I stand an atomic conglomerate,

Aware that the day will come for the takeover-

corporate,

When the asset strippers of Mother Nature PLC,

Will move in and dismantle all that made me,

And break everything down into those

valuable particles,

For the construction of new participating articles,

In the ongoing evolution of Life Industries PLC,

Eternity beckons for little old me!

GOD THE FATHER.

If a God was actually Jesus' dad,

would he really get so mad?

If someone with him didn't agree,

would he not perhaps, the other viewpoint see?

Do you think he'd look down from heaven's height,

and every non - Jew he saw he'd want to smite,

why would he on them want to jump,

and fire and brimstone on them dump?

Surely such havoc he would never wreak,

would he not just turn the other cheek?

IT IS WRITTEN!

In the darkness of the night,

a camp fire glows, yellow, orange, bright,

around it sit people who we now describe,

as together, having formed a tribe,

and as they roast their latest kill,

enough this time to eat their fill,

the father figure of them all,

begins to reminisce, yes, to recall,

stories of great deeds that he,

has stored within the recesses of his memory.

And through passing millennia it was thus done,

tribal histories passed from father to son,

until the populations of tribes had grown,

and many different stories had come to be known.

Then there came the great idea to draw,

depictions of what each day they saw,

when hunting the animals they needed to stay alive,

they recorded each species which then, did thrive,

painted on cave roof and wall,
wondrous visions which still enthral!

Change came slowly from this time, and,
populations moved to find new land,
so they could ensure their survival,
looking for space without any rival
tribes competing for scarce resources,
life was hard with Mother Nature's forces,
stacked against this new species, who,
compared to Earth's history, was brand new.

Successful tribes began to grow,
and with life experience they came to know,
that the hunter gatherer way of living,
was particularly hard, and unforgiving,
and that for their populations to expand,
they had to find new ways to exploit the land.
So from this point, change came faster,
sometimes punctuated by a natural disaster,
but change it did, and before too long,
they built settlements that were big, and strong,

on land from which they now knew,
the kind of crops from the soil best grew.

Agriculture now became widespread,
and meant that many more could be fed,
much time for many was now freed,
so towns grew larger, and so the need,
for new things that now could be made,
so with food surplus, came growth in trade,
as goods manufacture added worth,
sold to townsfolk who did not till the earth.

As trading increased with other tribes,
there grew a need for new ways to inscribe,
the dealings that took place each day,
to make sure buyers did the sellers pay.
This led to development from pictorial depiction,
to the earliest forms of inscription,
stone and clay tablets were at first employed,
and the new middle classes now enjoyed,
the great advances these changes brought,
as written language could now be taught.

Then tribal history, once passed paternally,

could now be written, and shared with all, eternally,

and legends from the peoples darkest past,

could be written in stone or clay, to last,

down through the ages they could now be read,

long after the ones who wrote these words, were dead.

This has meant that in our so called modern times,

we have seen the commission of unspeakable crimes,

because generations of 'scholars' have read
ancient scrolls,

and accepted as literal truth, what there unfolds,

instead of understanding these often called 'glories',

are merely the retelling of tribal camp fire stories.

TRULY ENTRANCED

He became a master of the fire dance,

His folk they followed without thinking,

Around the bonfires of wisdom, in a trance,

Thousands of torches through the darkness, twinkling.

The ancient symbols on banners unfurled,

Chosen as the new racial identity,

A rising crescendo of hatred was then hurled,

From the throat of this monstrous entity!

'Now I have you all in a trance,

You've joined me in my fire dance,

You made my fire burn even more bright,

By burning books to my great delight,

And so the scene is now set,

Most criteria have now been met,

I have already built the stage,

From which I can scream out my rage,

And I now see a global panorama,

Where I can now act out my drama,

In which millions are about to lose,

especially those sub-human Jews,

And Poles, and Slavs and Gypsies too,

They're going to see what we can do.

And as we purify the land,

For the greater good of the purest man,

Then the rest of the world will see,

You can't afford to mess with me.

And for all of you who accept the yoke,

Of total obedience, the chosen folk,

The Master Race, above all others,

Born of pure Arian fathers and mothers,

A thousand year Reich we will build,

Don't dare ask how many will be killed,

Because I know all, I am as God,

I hold in my hand the lightning rod,

To smite our enemies, all to kill,

For the Fatherland I will fulfil,

My plan for living space for you all,

As the sub-humans beneath us fall,

Fuel for our fires we will provide,

As we burn the millions who have died!'

BLIND FAITH

'You must believe my son,

you must let faith within you dwell,

because if you don't

you will doom your soul to everlasting Hell.'

Such were the words drummed into me

when I was eight or nine,

now here I am at fifty eight,

still waiting for a sign,

... some proof, a flash, a voice from god,

or something else divine.

Instead I have witnessed many other things,

solely from Earthly sources,

that tell me no compassionate god

could exude such malevolent forces,

surely a god that is good could never sit,

and watch so many die,

without sending angelic intervention,

a UN force from the sky!

Yet this has never happened

in the history of mankind,

through many thousands of years,

and many billions of tears,

the gods have always been deaf and blind!

'CURIOSITY' KILLED THE CAT!

We look up in wonder at the stars,

We ponder on there being life on Mars,

And so we've sent a craft to see,

A marvellous thing called 'Curiosity'.

And on the surface of the big red rock,

The last of its kind looks up in shock,

As from the sky there falls a star,

Which has travelled there from afar.

... Then the star begins to slow,

And the last Martian feline down below,

Stares in wonder, as a chute deploys,

Soon followed by the strangest noise,

As the thrusters ignite to stop,

The rapidity of the strange craft's drop.

And then the craft begins to lower,

A separate large object from below her,

Which lands upon the creature's head,

Leaving it squashed and very dead!

Now just how bloody ironic is that?

'Curiosity' killed the cat!

HUMAN O' WAR

What did you do in the war daddy?
Where did you fight, and who did you kill?
Were you a goody, or were you a baddy?
Did you join up against your will?

Or did you join to fight for pleasure,
to get a licence to take any life?
Was the body count how you would measure,
your success in the merciless strife?

Yes were you one who thought it such fun,
to shoot other human beings dead?
Did the power trip of carrying a gun,
drive all sense and reason from your head?

Perhaps the training you were given,
changed every point of view you held before.
Yes, all humanity from within you, driven,
to turn you into a dog of war.

And now you're home with your war ended,
will you settle into family life once more?
With all your nightmares and reality blended,
what does our future have in store?

LET US PREY

The Lord above, he came to me
and whispered in my ear,
'some folks down there, live their lives
in ignorance and fear,
so think how easy it would be to get them to pay,
to listen to you spoutin' off about me every day! '

So next mornin' at the crack o' dawn
I began my holy task,
by makin' sure that that first of all I would always ask,
my little congregation to pray real hard, then I'd holler,
that their prayers would work much better
if supported by their dollar.

Now gradually my following grew bigger day by day,
then I was asked on to TV to let more folks
hear me pray,

and now my preaching was on air every waking hour,

meaning that as my following grew,

therefore did my power.

I now own the votes of senators

and congressmen as well,

and if they don't do as I say,

then I'll make 'em go to hell,

'cos me and the Almighty have gotten us a pact,

that the gates of heaven will open,

to those who pay to join my act.

THE TRILOGY

If a child from birth is never told which religion

he must choose,

Will he belong to the Muslims,

the Christians or the Jews?

Or will he grow up using his brain as per natural

selection's design

To think for himself all through his life,

thus broadening his mind?

And if this way of doing things began to be widespread,

Would so many people in this world

still wind up being dead?

Long before their natural lives have run

their natural course,

Curtailed by some so called believer,

in an act of savage force!

Yes the fanatics use any means

to make us see the light,

But usually it is violence they employ

to prove that they are right.

Although, they never answer

any of the questions we raise,

They just tell us we must believe or die,

in the name of the imagined one they praise!

THE ALMIGHTY ATOM!

Everything including me,

Is made of atoms that came to be,

With the explosion of a star,

Light years away from where we are,

And then these atoms pulled together,

And formed our planet and the British weather,

And eventually, the human brain,

Which despite obsessing about the rain,

Could probe creation using math,

And work out a theorem in the bath!

So did the atoms somehow decide,

That they alone, could never provide,

Any answers for any questions asked,

So they made an intelligence which could be tasked,

With providing answers as to how,

Atoms came to take their bow?

THE TRICKSTERS

The clever magician will have us believe,

that he keeps nothing up his sleeve,

that none of what he does is tricks,

that all of it is a pure mix,

of miracles that he creates,

and from thin air, substance, emanates.

The clever politician plays a similar game,

like the magician he will claim,

that from thin air he can produce,

the things with which he can seduce,

whole populations for him to vote,

at your next election, please take note!

U N Happiness

I am living in Bhutan,

and I am a very happy man!

At least that's what they say I am!

No one came to ask me though,

so how is it that they could know

that I am such a contented chap?

Now this has got me in a flap,

to find that the UN in the USA,

has now come up with some way,

to tell how happy we all are,

they must have scanned me from afar!

And by doing this they've read my mind,
which is a very scary thing to find,
and just by listening to the BBC,
I know I've had this done to me!
So now I fear all the time,
that I'm a victim of cyber crime.
They stole the happiness I had,
and left me full of fear, and sad!

ULTIMATELY WE'RE ALL GREEN

They say it's easier to die if you've got nowt,

so little that's good to leave behind!

But for the wealthy it must be much harder,

with all that comfort and luxury in mind.

The poor are taught to expect zero,

and that is just what they get,

the rich all have great expectations,

and they all know that these will be met.

So all through Life's divided journey,

the contrast is massive, and stark.

There are those who thrive in the sunshine,

and those who wither in the dark.

But in the end we all become equal,

and money means nothing at all,

when you're returned to the earth and recycled,

the main course at the ugly bug ball!

SUFFER NOT THE LITTLE CHILDREN?

Mercy, Mercy Lord above,
I am begging of you please,
I pray oh Lord that in your love,
you will, my pain and suffering ease.

Again oh Lord, Almighty one,
please listen to my pleading,
before all hope within me is gone,
please stop my people's bleeding.

Oh mighty one, for many days,
I have prayed to you to help me,
please use your divine and miraculous ways,
to save us, and bring back my daddy!

Oh mighty Lord of all mankind,
again I beg you to intervene.
Please my God, please don't be blind,

please see what all the world has seen.

The soldiers, they come every day,
they shell and shoot, and spare no one.
We try to hide, we all still pray,
but my faith in prayer has now gone.

So if you are there, can I ask,
a question, oh mighty invisible Lord?
Why do you never take to task,
those who live and rule by the sword?

Our Time

Thinker,

Failure,

Soldier,

Sailor,

Airman,

Dead man,

Grief.

Politician,

Preacher,

Blind man,

Teacher,

Banker,

Usurer,

Thief.

ME AND MY SHADOW

A big black dog is following me,

Everywhere I go,

I don't know where it came from,

But it just seems to grow.

Every time I look at it,

It gets bigger, and more black.

I cannot make it go away,

It just will not turn back!

I close my eyes and make a wish,

But my wish is never granted,

And I feel I am just a fish,

Taken from the water, and supplanted,

Into a hostile environment,

Where it's impossible to survive,

How long can I suffer this,

Do I want to stay alive?

PEN VERSUS SWORD

Who did any writer ever save?
When did words raise anyone from the grave?
Never has the great mind through writing
Put an end to war and fighting.
Ideas like icebergs, drift then melt
And through time no change is ever felt.
Because shortly after publication
Of their high ideals, and their computation,
Of why mankind just loves killing
Still so many are oh so willing
To join the disparate armies of the world
As soon as the flags have been unfurled.
No matter that so many have already died
They wear the team colours with such pride,
And march off to the tune played by the piper

Paid for by the profit driven viper

Who wraps his coils around the nation,

As history screams in absolute frustration

That out of nothing the men of war

Have created a cause, worth dying for!

FATTY BUM BUM

How did I end up in this state?
I'm always fighting with my weight,
I'd like to put it down to fate,
but that ain't honest!

I know for sure what I do wrong,
I've known the truth all along,
but I always sing a different song,
and that ain't honest!

I've tried to blame my family,
for passing the fat gene down to me,
and making me a big fat 'B',
but that ain't honest.

So now I'm gonna face the fact,
I have to make me a slimming pact,
and with exercise I must react.
Now, that is honest!

Learn Or Burn?

I am human just like you

Arms and legs, two and two

Eyes and ears, two as well,

And one nose with which to smell.

The only differences I can detect,

Are the ways we use our intellects.

There are those who believe

There are those who think

There are those who believe they think

There are those who think that they believe,

And those who simply can't conceive

Of anything other than what they've been told

Are they incapable of being, just a little bit bold?

And questioning that which they've been taught

Perhaps even introducing an original thought.

So if you think for yourself do not condemn
Life should not be a game of us and them,
The aim should be to educate,
To enlighten minds, not to berate.
We should communicate in a civilised fashion,
About that which arouses so much passion.
So perhaps with time some may think
For themselves and break the link.
Because from our history we should have learned,
That once the books start being burned,
It isn't long before we see,
Those with whom the fire raisers disagree
Replacing books to fuel the fire
The re-ignition of that vast funeral pyre!

How?

If before the big bang there was nought.
How come the prophets and philosophers
never thought
To raise a major point, strangely missed,
That before the universe, time did not exist!

So if there was no such thing as time
Is it not just a bit asinine
to state categorically that a god is the creator,
was he there before, or did he come later?

Yes how did such a deity come to be,
in order to make you and me,
the universe, the stars, the planets, all lands and seas?
Answers on a postcard, please!

Live Or Diet!

Well, here it is, and here I am
For dinner a lettuce leaf, and a slice of ham.
If this tiny morsel, on this great big plate
Is supposed to ensure that I lose weight.

Then rest assured, it will ensue,
That pounds will drop off, and not just a few.
No, if I stick to this, then let it be known
That I'm gonna wind up skin and bone.

My body parts will shrivel and waste,
And to top it all, I can't even taste
Such a teeny weeny piece of food,
If I served this to guest, I would be rude.

So I am going to make an increase to
My slices of ham, yes, that's what I'll do,
A tasty four slices I'll have of ham,
And frankly my dear I don't give a damn.

That this may slow my weight loss down,
As it will help to rid me of this frown,
And also I'll add another three
Lettuce leaves 'cos they're good for me,

And then perhaps a tomato or two,
To enhance the flavour, yes this I'll do.
Then some nice wedges of mature cheese
Which will my waiting taste buds please.

Then to top it all, and add mucho taste,

In a sweet chilli dressing, the lot I'll baste,

Then I'll pile it all between hunks of buttered bread,

Because I intend to live before I'm dead!

And if I stick to this, then I'll never be known,

As skinny Tom, the human xylophone!

BATTLE CRY OF THE REPUBLICANS!

'Believe me folks, when I say,

That I know exactly which way,

This country needs to go,

In order for the economy to grow.

And, unlike the incumbent there,

My friends and I, we really care,

About the direction that this great nation,

Needs to take, and, indeed, the frustration,

That we know you folks out there are feeling,

We're here for you, and we're appealing,

For your valuable votes, so that we,

Can take you where we want you to be.

And working with our friends at Haliburton,

You can rest assured, yes you can be certain,

That everything will go as planned,

Directed by God's almighty hand.

We aren't going to tell you just now,

That you will all have to pay, and how!

When we take on the mullahs of Iran,

And attack them from Afghanistan! '

Count Your Blessings

Often circumstances can conspire

To make a life's experience dire.

If this should ever happen to you,

This is what you ought to do.

Look around yourself to see,

If there is a worse place you could be,

And usually you'll find 'tis so,

There's somewhere worse where you could go,

And the poor beggars dwelling there,

Have many more woes about which to care,

So count your blessings and sing in praise.

You're better off than them, oh happy days!

POPPY PRICE TAG

' In Flanders fields the poppies blow,

Between the crosses, row on row'.

So wrote the poet John McCrae,

Recording the reality of his day.

Now after ninety four years have gone,

The use of the poppy has now moved on.

Instead of remembrance of the brave,

It sends addicted millions to an early grave,

And today our young troops fight and die,

Without anyone asking the real question, why?

In Helmand's fields the poppies blow,

Beside the compounds where they grow,

Surrounded by hidden IED's,

Planted to kill and maim with ease,

The brave young men sent on patrol,

Hoping they return alive and whole,

As they risk all to do their duty,

The poppy crop provides illicit booty,

That funds the continuation of this war,

In which no one can say what we're fighting for!

HINDSIGHT

Ooh! I want to be creative,

yes I want to make my mark,

Yes I need to leave my indent

like the bite of a great white shark!

I'm sick of not being noticed, fed up with going unseen.

Just one more of all of those who never,

ever have been.

There must be more to my being here,

a good reason I exist,

It can't all be down to waiting for the next time

we get pissed!

I know when I was young I had a natural bent,

For doing things artistically,

but that would not pay the rent,

So I did what I did not want to do

and joined the rats at play,

And plodded on the treadmill for eight hours every day.

And now so many years have passed
and my treading carries on,
But I have never found my Shangri La and soon
I will be gone.
Without the joy of having made the life I really yearned,
Too late to take advantage of a lesson cruelly learned.

So be brave and strong you youngsters if you are
nurturing a skill,
Don't let the pressure to pay the rent
drive you onto that mill.
Open your mind, open your eyes,
Develop your talent and reach for the skies,
Soar like a bird and find your own way,
And don't eat the crumbs from the trap called payday!

A Real Recession.

Because of this recession, how badly hit I am!
I now must eat more chicken
and cut right down on lamb.
Oh how we're all affected,
and for some it seems quite bad
But if you put it in perspective it makes me really sad,

That here we are all a whingeing
and bemoaning our lot,
When we really should be singing
to give thanks for a still full pot.
While out there in the other world,
their reality they must face,
Each night they lie in hunger curled,
so many others of our race.

Because the lottery of life

condemns them to such a fate,

Nothing but fear, hunger and strife

to make up their daily plate.

So how damaged are we really?

Those of us in the West,

Always so indifferent ,

whilst living on the best

Gobbling up resources produced in the poorest parts

Eating multiple courses and swelling

our fat filled hearts.

While out there in forgotten lands

the people waste away

Reaching out with bony hands that can't afford to pay,

To have the basic needs of life
that we all take for granted
With exploitation and corruption rife,
against them life is slanted,
To make it so hard for them all to ever find a way
To clamber up and over the wall
to start anew their day.

So how poor are we really? How forgotten and forlorn,
Are our clothes merely tatters
or are our shoes totally worn?
Do our children cry with hunger
or die of curable disease?
Are we thirsting for clean water,
or are we begging on our knees?

Of course we know the answer
and it is really hard to face,
That for us to grow and prosper
we impoverish others of our race.
So when you rise each morning and get ready
to start your day,
Count your blessings that the dawning finds you where
you want to stay.

In this green old land of plenty
where the children laugh and play,
Because their plates are never empty,
and where all can have a say
In the way they want to live their lives without
constantly being in fear
Of discussing any subject that those
in power don't want to hear!

I'M IN CHARGE.

I am a very pious and god fearing man,

I currently command the Taliban,

And I am doing all I can,

To clear the Infidel from Afghanistan.

To do this every day I will,

Kafirs at every opportunity, kill,

By any method I can find,

Developed by my poisoned mind.

And when at last they have all gone,

I'll promote myself to number one,

And I'll decide who'll live or die,

I will the Shari-ah law apply,

To all who don't do as I say,

They will not live another day.

We will hang, stone, shoot or behead,

All who I say needs to be dead!

And those, If any, who question why,

Will join the lists of those to die.

So kneel with me and praise the great lord,

For showing me how mighty is his sword!

An Older Version Of Me!

I'm getting older,

A bit less bolder,

About risk physical

I'm getting stronger,

As I live longer,

About risk lyrical.

I'm going to be ruthless,

As I grow toothless,

And say what I am thinking.

I'm going to defend,

As I approach the end,

Free speech from ever sinking!

BRING ME SUNSHINE

The sun shone down on all those vines,

And worked with their chlorophyll

To produce the sugars to fill the grapes

That make wine for me and Gill!

So that we can stay in on Saturdays

And enjoy a drink whilst we watch TV

A sad existence I must admit

When we would much rather be

Out socialising at the Tow Bar Inn

Like we did when we were young.

But now there's nowhere left to match

The place that provided such fun!

So most Saturday nights we sit and watch
The would be stars all trying
To win the votes to be rated high
And not have to walk off crying!

But life as most of us will learn
Blends kindness with being cruel
And many who think they're great
Are made to look the fool!

GLOBALISM UNFOLDING

I own you! You will obey me,

And for owning you, you will pay me.

You will work for me all of your days

Your choices limited to whatever I say.

You are mine, I own you!

You'll be just fine, another clone to

Be utilised with all the others

All of who are trained, just like your mothers,

And your fathers too

To be obedient, and always do

Everything I tell you to.

I own you!

I own each and every politician.

You may think they're on a mission,

But I have bought the whole damn crew

To ensure my ownership of you!

I own the police, I own the law,

I own everything you think is worth fighting for.

I own the judges of the supreme court,

They come with the politicians I bought.

I own the schools, I own the teachers,

I own the churches and the preachers,

I own the kids and what they're learning,

I own what little money folks are earning.

I own the media, it says what I say,

I own you, and you will obey!

I own nearly it all, ninety nine percent!

I own you in your ragged tent,

I left you all with barely a cent,

I own you!

I own the farms, I own the mills,

I own gigantic companies making pills,

I own the treatments to make you well,

But if you're poor you can go to hell!

I own the shops and all they sell,

And I even own good old Santa Clause.

I own the marvellous armament producers,

And all the vicious wars they cause.

I own the means of all production,

I own the button of mass destruction,

I own the army in which you serve,

Join up, and you'll get what you deserve.

I own the air force and the navy too,

But there's still so much for me to do.

I own you!

I look up at night and see the stars

So pretty soon I will own Mars.

I have great control over how you think,

I own the water that you drink.

I'll get my media to have you believe

That it's fine for me to own the air you breathe.

I own the means of keeping you warm,

I own every port in calm or storm.

I own the land where your ancestors lie,

I own all of the space that you occupy.

I own Mother Nature, the seas and the sky,

And I will own all of you until you die!

So come on y'all and give up your thanks

For the future prosperity of me and my banks!

I own you!

GONE FISHING

They launched at dawn, Jim and his mate,
both men unaware of their mutual fate.
The boat was small, the sea was calm,
and neither of them foresaw any harm.

This was something both had done,
at the rising of the sun
on many, many previous days,
they'd sailed out into the haze.

This time it seemed just the same,
the weather was mild, the wind was tame,
though neither of these good friends could know,
just how this trip was destined to go.

Before they left home they checked the weather,
the forecast was fine, and they laughed together,
because today was perfect for their trip,
so they headed down to the launching slip.

At last they were headed out to sea,

for this much anticipated fishing spree,

all bait and tackle at the ready,

their progress out at first was steady.

About six miles out from their home port,

lies a mark from which they had caught,

a lot of fish, over lots of years,

but back on shore there would soon be tears.

At three miles out, suddenly,

a thick mist rolled across the sea,

and rapidly they were so fogbound,

that they feared they would never be found.

Their boat was fine in sight of land,

but lost in fog, they'd never planned,

for such an eventuality,

blind with no compass, miles out at sea.

They slowed the boat so they could hear,

if any other craft came near,

when suddenly out of the gloom,

appeared the harbinger of their doom.

A ship so huge they could not steer,

beyond the bow so high and sheer,

as it bore down on them at a hellish rate,

and sliced their boat, and sealed their fate.

The great ship passed on as no one knew

that they'd just killed the small boat's crew,

and back on shore it was not yet known

that both of the friends would never come home.

By eight that night they began to worry,

and to the launching slip they did hurry.

They called the coastguard, and he,

called on all shipping in the vicinity.

After hours of searching from lifeboat, and sky,
and many other vessels that were passing by.
Nothing was found, out in the mist,
it seemed the men did not exist.

And this of course, was totally true
the men had sunk down into the deep blue,
they were lost at sea without a trace,
departed from the human race.

Printed in Great Britain
by Amazon

35671428R00071